BY JESSICA GUNDERSON

PRESIDENT McKINLEY'S KILLER AND THE AMERICA HE LEFT BEHIND

THE ASSASSIN, THE CRIME, TEDDY ROOSEVELT'S RISE, AND THE DAWN OF THE AMERICAN CENTURY

COMPASS POINT BOOKS
a capstone imprint

For my husband, Jason, who has spent many Saturday afternoons watching historical documentaries with me, and who shares my interest in presidential history. —JG

Special thanks to our consultant, Christopher Kenney, Director of Education, McKinley Presidential Library & Museum, for his guidance.

Assassins' America is published by Compass Point Books, a Capstone imprint
1710 Roe Crest Drive, North Mankato, Minnesota 56003
www.mycapstone.com

Library of Congress Cataloging-in-Publication Data
Names: Gunderson, Jessica, author.
Title: President McKinley's killer and the America he left behind : the assassin, the crime, Teddy Roosevelt's rise, and the dawn of the American century / by Jessica Gunderson.
Description: North Mankato, Minnesota : Compass Point Books, 2018. |
Series: Assassins' America | Audience: Ages 9-15.
Identifiers: LCCN 2017042673 (print) | LCCN 2017043548 (ebook) | ISBN 9780756557225 (eBook pdf) | ISBN 9780756557140 (hardcover) | ISBN 9780756557188 (pbk.)
Subjects: LCSH: McKinley, William, 1843-1901—Assassination—Juvenile literature. | Czolgosz, Leon F., 1873?-1901—Juvenile literature.
Classification: LCC E711.9 (ebook) | LCC E711.9 .G86 2018 (print) | DDC 973.88092—dc23
LC record available at https://lccn.loc.gov/2017042673

Editorial Credits
Nick Healy, editor; Mackenzie Lopez and Kay Fraser, designers; Svetlana Zhurkin, media researcher; Tori Abraham, production specialist

Printed and bound in the United States of America.
010749S18

TABLE OF CONTENTS

Leon Czolgosz, assassin

CHAPTER 1
McKINLEY'S KILLER

The time is the summer of 1901, and the World's Fair is in full swing. Millions of people descend upon Delaware Park in Buffalo, New York, to see the new inventions on display and to enjoy the fair's festivities. Colorful buildings glisten in the sunlight. Canals and waterways meander through the park. Rosebushes line the walkways. But the fair is most spectacular at night, when the grounds and the fair's major attraction — the 389-foot Electric Tower — light up. Crowds ooh and ahh at the sight. It is the early years of electricity, and no one has seen so many lights before. Glowing bulbs line every building and every walkway. The place feels magical. The fair at night transforms into a city of light.

On September 5 another blaze of light spreads across the sky. This time it is brilliant fireworks. And the fireworks spell out a message: Welcome, President McKinley! Chief of Our Nation and Our Empire!

President McKinley addresses a large crowd at the World's Fair.

President William McKinley is on a two-day visit to the World's Fair. He's just several months into his second term as president. He's enjoying enormous popularity after leading the United States to a speedy victory in the Spanish-American War and acquiring the territories of Guam, Puerto Rico, and the Philippines. The World's Fair is called the Pan-American Exposition to celebrate the new territories under U.S. control.

More than 116,000 people gather on the fairgrounds to listen to the president speak. "Expositions are the timekeepers of progress," he says. Crowds cheer during the speech, and he calls for "prosperity, happiness and peace to all our neighbors, and like blessings to all the peoples and powers of earth."

Another roar rises from the crowd, but not everyone is cheering. Zoom in and look at the audience more closely. Standing near the president's podium is a young man, scowling. His face darkens at McKinley's every word. And if you zoom in even closer, you may notice that he has one hand in his pocket. Fingering his gun.

Who is this man with the searing hatred for McKinley? His name is Leon Czolgosz. (That last name is difficult. Here's a simple way to pronounce it: CHOLE-GOSH.) He has a complicated life story but a simple plan. He intends to shoot and kill McKinley. But the beginning of his story — and of his troubles — goes back more than three decades.

Leon Czolgosz was a factory worker who'd led a hardworking life as the son of poor Polish immigrants. He was born in Alpena, Michigan, in 1873. He was one of eight children. His father, Paul, worked hauling lumber on the docks of Lake Huron, making only 30 cents an hour (about $5 an hour in today's money). For four months of the year, he was laid off by the lumber company. He made so little money that the family could barely survive.

When Leon was about 5 years old, the Czolgosz family bought a farm. They were happier on the farm, even though they still had to work hard. But a few years later, tragedy shook the family. Leon's mother, Mary, died in childbirth. Without Mary to take care of the household, Paul decided to move the family back to Alpena, where he could find work. Over the next several years, the family moved around — Michigan to Pennsylvania to Ohio. The Czolgosz children worked in factories and on farms to help support the family. Leon worked too. When he was a young teenager, he got his first job at a glassworks factory near Pittsburgh, Pennsylvania.

Was it even legal for children to work in factories? At that time, the answer was yes. Only a few states had laws against child labor. Factories were happy to hire children. Children had a lot of energy. Plus, factories could pay kids a lot less than adults. And for struggling families, any income a child brought home would help. The situation worked out for everybody — everybody except the children. Days spent working in factories were long, exhausting,

Children working in a cotton mill, 1909

and dangerous. Children suffered and toiled all day just to bring home a few cents. Imagine if, instead of sending you off to school each morning, your parents sent you to work at a canning plant or a textile mill. And bear in mind that at the end of a long day, you would have to give all the money you earned to your parents to help feed your siblings. That was the case for millions of American children in the late 1800s and early 1900s.

So Leon spent part of his childhood working. Somehow he continued his schooling until he was 16, which was unusual for poor immigrant children, most of whom dropped out and went to work earlier. Leon's brothers said that he was a good student, so his family didn't take him out of school to work full time.

When the Czolgosz family moved to Cleveland, Ohio, Leon got a job at a wire mill, making steel wire for fences. But in 1893 the U.S. economy collapsed. Wages dropped. Workers at the wire factory went on strike to demand fairer treatment. Leon joined them in the walkout. The wire company responded by firing every worker who'd gone on strike.

Out of work, 20-year-old Leon struggled to make sense of the world. He believed in the American dream. And he'd always been interested in American society and its ups and downs. So he started reading a lot. First he read the Bible front to back. He stopped attending church because he felt the priests left out the most important parts of the Bible.

Then he read a book called *Looking Backward* by Edward Bellamy. The novel is about a man named Julian West who goes to sleep in 1887 and wakes up in the year 2000. In the story's version of the future, social classes do not fight with each other but instead work together. The novel struck a chord with Czolgosz. He was upset by the way the poor were treated by the wealthy upper class. He felt the wealthy took advantage of the poor. And he concluded that the wealthy and poor should work together to make life better for everyone.

Six months after being fired, Leon decided to try to get his job back at the wire mill. He knew he was on a list of strikers who'd been dismissed. His old boss, however, had moved on. The new boss wouldn't recognize him. So Czolgosz walked in the door and introduced himself as Fred Nieman. Fred was a family nickname for him. Nieman was easier to pronounce than Czolgosz, and it means "nobody" in German. His scheme worked. He got his job back.

Around this time Leon started joining groups that talked about social issues. He grew increasingly upset by the low wages that his job offered. He hated how big businesses made money but workers remained poor. He hated capitalism, which allowed the gap between rich and poor to widen.

His life was soon disrupted by illness. He couldn't breathe very well, and his heart kept beating rapidly. He visited doctors several times and took several medications that didn't seem to help. No one knows what illnesses he suffered from — or whether they were real or imagined. In 1898 he quit his job. He holed up in his family's house, barely speaking to anyone, especially not his stepmother. He spent his time sleeping and reading publications about politics and social issues. Isolated and ill, the young Czolgosz developed an interest in anarchy, an idea that seemed to fascinate political outsiders and downtrodden people in that era.

What is anarchy? The word is Greek for "no ruler." Anarchy is basically belief in a society without government or law. Anarchists in Czolgosz's time railed against governments and monarchies (nations run by kings and queens).

The ideas of anarchy were exciting to Leon. He became especially interested in the lectures and writings of Emma Goldman. She was a Russian immigrant living

Emma Goldman

in the United States and a strong supporter of anarchy. She gave passionate, fiery speeches against authority. Her speeches drew crowds of thousands. Leon went to Chicago to one of her speeches. In that speech she stated that anarchists must gain their goals by intelligence, not by violence. But then she said that violence was sometimes understandable. Sometimes people couldn't sit around while wrongs were inflicted upon them.

Anarchists like Emma Goldman believed that all authority should be eliminated. And, in the 1890s, some anarchists started taking matters into their own hands. A string of killings and other violent events played out in Europe and North America:

1886, Haymarket Square, Chicago. Culprit: unknown. Crime: Someone throws a bomb at Chicago police, who are there

Haymarket Square riot in Chicago, 1886

to break up a workers' protest. Death toll: Seven police officers, four civilians. Convicted: Eight anarchists.

1893, Spain. Culprit: Santiago Salvador, anarchist. Crime: Salvador throws explosives into a theater filled with rich people. Death toll: About 20.

1893, France. Culprit: Auguste Vaillant, anarchist. Crime: Vaillant throws a small bomb into the French Parliament. No one is killed, but Vaillant is executed for the deed. Vaillant's last words: "Long live anarchy!"

1894, Lyons, France. Culprit: Cesare Santo, anarchist. Crime: Santo wraps a newspaper around a dagger. He approaches the carriage of French president Sadi Carnot and stabs him. Death toll: One — Sadi Carnot.

1897, Spain. Culprit: Michele Angiolillo, anarchist. Crime: Angiolillo goes to a bath resort where Spanish prime minister Canovas del Castillo is staying and shoots him. Death toll: One — Canovas del Castillo.

1898, Switzerland. Culprit: Luigi Lucheni, anarchist. Lucheni walks up to Empress Elisabeth of Austria and pretends to stumble into her. He stabs her with a concealed knife. Death toll: One — Empress Elisabeth.

These violent acts frightened citizens worldwide. But Leon Czolgosz was not frightened. Instead he was fascinated. To him, violence seemed the only way to bring down unfair systems of government. Czolgosz believed the words of German anarchist Johann Most, who said, "Violence is justified against tyranny and tyrants."

In the spring of 1898, protests erupted in Italy over the rising price of bread. King Umberto I silenced the protests by placing the country under military control. The military fired a cannon into a crowd in Milan, killing more than 100 people.

Far away in New Jersey, an Italian immigrant and anarchist named Gaetano Bresci heard about the massacre. Enraged, he plotted to somehow kill the king. He said goodbye to his family and set off for Italy.

On July 29, 1900, King Umberto had just gotten into his royal carriage when a tall man pushed through the crowd. The man

The assassination of Italy's King Umberto I was part of a wave of political violence.

was Gaetano Bresci, all the way from New Jersey. Bresci drew his pistol and fired three shots at the surprised king. Umberto died, and Bresci was arrested.

In Ohio, Leon Czolgosz read of King Umberto's assassination in the newspaper. He carefully cut out the article and folded it into his wallet. Umberto's murder had given him an idea — a deadly, gruesome idea that would change America's future. He decided that he, too, would take matters into his own hands. He would kill President William McKinley.

William McKinley won election in 1896 and reelection in 1900.

CHAPTER 2
A POPULAR PRESIDENT

Who was William McKinley? What did he do to incur such wrath? He was a popular president, so why did Leon Czolgosz feel the desire to kill him? Did McKinley deserve blame for the trouble of the poor and jobless? Or did he just happen to be in the wrong place at the wrong time? Was he a mere symbol of the government that anarchists wanted to bring down?

William McKinley was born in 1843 in Niles, Ohio, to a middle-class family. Niles was a rural town, and young William loved to roam the nearby woods, slosh about in Mosquito Creek, and fly his kite. He attended school in a one-room schoolhouse. He was a hardworking student and always wanted to be at the top of his class. He attended college briefly and then became a schoolteacher. Then the Civil War began.

McKinley admired President Abraham Lincoln, and, guided by strong patriotism, he enlisted in the Union Army. Leaving behind his days as a teacher, McKinley quickly became a skilled soldier and was promoted to commissary sergeant. In this role he was in charge of feeding the troops. September 1862 saw the bloodiest one-day battle of the war — the Battle of Antietam. McKinley's unit arrived hours after the battle started. The Union soldiers, just over the hill, were hungry and thirsty. To reach them with supplies, McKinley would have to ride right through the battle. The danger was clear, but he was determined. As bullets whizzed and cannons blasted, McKinley raced his wagon directly into enemy fire. The Union soldiers cheered as McKinley and the wagon of goods arrived, somehow unharmed.

One man took particular notice of McKinley's bravery. That man was Rutherford B. Hayes, a senior officer in McKinley's regiment. Hayes became a mentor to McKinley. After the war McKinley became a lawyer, and he aspired to become involved in politics. Hayes helped McKinley's budding political career, and they both ended up in Washington, D.C. Hayes was sworn in as U.S. president in 1877, and McKinley became one of Ohio's representatives in the U.S. Congress. As a lawmaker he authored the McKinley Tariff, which put a high tax on imported goods. The tax was meant to protect U.S. industry from foreign competitors.

McKinley married Ida Saxton in 1871, and the couple had two daughters. One died as a baby, and the other died at age 3. The children's deaths sent Ida into a deep depression. She never recovered. She also developed epilepsy, a condition that causes seizures. McKinley was devoted to her and constantly tended to her.

McKinley's devotion to his wife was one quality that made voters love him. After running as a Republican (the party of

The McKinley campaign promised to boost the U.S. economy and raise the country's stature around the world.

Lincoln), he served as the governor of Ohio from 1892 to 1896. In 1896 he ran for president of the United States.

McKinley's campaign for president was backed by "big money." His supporters included multimillionaires such as Andrew Carnegie and John D. Rockefeller. His opponent, Democrat William Jennings Bryan, campaigned for the working class. But McKinley also could proclaim his support for the working class. As governor he had protected worker safety and workers' unions.

McKinley did all his campaigning from his home. He sat on his front porch in Canton, Ohio, giving speeches and welcoming visitors. He made himself available to voters every day of the week except Sunday. The economic crash of 1893 had weakened the U.S. economy and put many people out of work. McKinley promised to further tax all goods imported from other countries. This, he promised, would help American industries grow.

McKinley won the election by a wide margin. He immediately set about trying to repair the economy. His business-friendly presidency helped "trusts" to develop. A trust is a large combination of corporations. Because there is little or no competition, trusts can charge high prices for their products. They can make a heap of money this way. The Standard Oil Company was one trust that had bought out most of its smaller competitors and gained almost complete control of oil production and sale.

You can see why McKinley's ideas would upset poor, working-class Americans like Leon Czolgosz. But large corporations also employed lots of people and helped the economy. Plus, McKinley's import taxes helped American industries, putting people back to work.

And something else was about to make McKinley more popular — a victorious war.

At the time Cuba was in trouble. Since 1895 Cuba had been engaged in a struggle for independence from Spain. Across the United States, newspapers told of the horrific measures the Spanish were using to put down the rebellion. Hundreds of thousands of civilians were forced from their homes. Many Americans thought the United States should help Cuba fight for independence. Plus the United States would gain Spain's territories if the U.S. won, making the nation more powerful. President McKinley,

The damaged USS Maine

however, was hesitant to go to war with Spain. He resisted calls to fight until the U.S. naval ship USS *Maine* mysteriously exploded and sank in a Cuban harbor.

McKinley had sent the USS *Maine* to Havana, Cuba, to ensure the safety of American citizens there. On the night of February 15, 1898, an explosion ripped through the front of the ship. The USS *Maine* sank quickly. More than 260 American seamen died.

No one knew what caused the explosion. But many people thought Spain was to blame. Calls for war grew louder, and this time, McKinley listened. In April he sent troops to Cuba in support of its independence. On April 25 the United States Congress officially declared war on Spain.

The fighting didn't last long. Spain was not very well prepared, and its military was soundly defeated at Manila Bay in the Philippines and at San Juan Hill in Santiago, Cuba. And, after the war, one soldier emerged as a hero — a man named Theodore Roosevelt.

Roosevelt was the Assistant Secretary of the Navy and a strong supporter of going to war with Spain. When the fighting began, Roosevelt resigned from his job in order to organize a volunteer regiment. He gathered men from the southwest United States. He figured they were used to a hot climate like what they would encounter in Cuba. He enlisted ranchers, cowboys, gamblers, American Indians, college athletes, and hunters. The group was varied, but they all had a few things in common: They were sharpshooters and skilled horseback riders. The regiment was dubbed the Rough Riders.

Clad in blue flannel shirts, brown pants, boots, and slouchy

Theodore Roosevelt was eager to join the fighting in the Spanish-American War.

hats, 1,060 Rough Riders set off for Cuba. They landed near the Spanish-held city of Santiago and advanced on the city. On July 1, 1898, Roosevelt himself led the Rough Riders on a dramatic charge. The Spanish retreated, and just a few days later, they surrendered.

The Treaty of Paris, signed in December, officially ended the war. Cuba gained its independence, and Spain signed over Guam and Puerto Rico to the United States. The treaty also allowed the U.S. to purchase the Philippines. With control of these islands in the Caribbean Sea and far off in the Pacific, the United States was now an empire.

Riding high on the successes in his first term, McKinley entered the election of 1900 feeling confident. His vice president, Garret Hobart, had died in late 1899, so McKinley would need a new running mate to share the Republican 1900 ticket. The Republican Party chose the Rough Rider hero, Theodore Roosevelt.

And who was McKinley up against? His opponent was the same as in the last election, William Jennings Bryan.

"McKinley Was Right!" a campaign poster proclaimed. McKinley's message focused on the economic growth the nation had experienced during his first term, as well as the worldwide admiration by winning the Spanish-American War. "Prosperity at home, prestige abroad!" was McKinley's slogan. With Roosevelt, he had a national war hero at his side to emphasize his successes and promote his ideas.

McKinley won once again, crushing William Jennings Bryan in the count of electoral votes. He entered his second term with high hopes. A new century was underway. The Buffalo World's

Fair — held in the summer and autumn of 1901 — celebrated the U.S. victory over Spain and the dawning of the American empire. A fireworks display arced across the sky, welcoming McKinley to Buffalo.

As he spoke to the crowd, President McKinley had no idea that not everyone was happy to see him. He did not suspect that one man in the masses meant to kill him.

Giant steel factories became a symbol of the Industrial Revolution.

CHAPTER 3
TIMES OF CHANGE

In the last half of the 1800s, industrial growth spread across the United States. This period was known as the American Industrial Revolution. New railroads crossed the country from the Atlantic Ocean to the Pacific. People no longer had to travel long distances in wagons pulled by beasts of burden. They could travel more quickly from one place to another. People could also connect with others far away without traveling at all, after Alexander Graham Bell invented the telephone in 1876. A few years later, Thomas Edison perfected his light bulb. In the following years, electric lights sparkled in the windows of houses and buildings. Street lamps glowed, lighting the way.

More startling and life-changing inventions followed. The first automobiles were produced in the 1870s and 1880s. Although automobiles didn't become widely made or used until the early 1900s, everyone knew big changes in transportation were coming.

Other innovations included motion pictures (also known as movies), which awed crowds at public screenings.

Perhaps one of the most important changes that affected many Americans came in manufacturing. Before the Industrial Revolution, most goods were made at home or at small home businesses, using hand tools or small hand-powered machines. The process was slow. But the invention of large machines, powered by steam engines, moved manufacturing of goods to big factories. Goods could be produced quickly and in large quantities. Textile mills sprang up throughout the northeastern United States in the mid-1800s. Other mills and factories followed, making paper, iron, steel, clocks, weapons, and many other goods.

People streamed from rural areas into cities to work in factories. The urban population surged. Men, women, children — anyone could work at a factory. But the work wasn't easy. Factory workers toiled long hours for low wages. Many workers, especially women, returned home from a grueling day of work only to face more work — cooking, cleaning, and caring for children.

Often the children who worked in factories were given dangerous jobs. Because kids were small, they could crawl into huge machines to clean them. Children could also wiggle into mines and small areas where adults couldn't fit. And children were paid very little, sometimes not at all. By 1900, 18 percent of all American laborers were under the age of 16. That means nearly one of every five workers was a kid.

During the Industrial Revolution, waves and waves of immigrants poured into the United States. Most of these immigrants worked in factories. Between 1860 and 1900, 14 million immigrants came to

Many workers lived in crowded urban neighborhoods such as New York City's Little Italy.

the United States. The Czolgosz family was one such immigrant family.

Factory workers didn't take home much money. But factory owners did. Consider Andrew Carnegie, for example. In the 1870s he started a steel mill in Pennsylvania. He bought out his rival, Homestead Steel, and formed the Carnegie Steel Company. Then he owned most of the steel operations in the United States. He became one of the richest men in America.

Rivaling Carnegie as the richest man in America was John D. Rockefeller. Rockefeller bought an oil company and later formed Standard Oil, which grew to a staggering size. Standard Oil bought out smaller oil companies and became a powerful trust. Soon Rockefeller controlled 90 percent of the nation's oil.

Andrew Carnegie

Were men like Carnegie and Rockefeller bad men, rolling in riches while their workers suffered and toiled for low wages? That's something people still disagree about. In fact, both men had started from the bottom, working for little pay at factories, eventually climbing their way up. When Carnegie finally sold his steel company for $480 million (that's equal to about $13.8 billion today), he gave away almost all of it. His money built museums and libraries around the country.

Some people admired Carnegie and Rockefeller for their rags-to-riches stories. After all, hadn't they achieved the American dream? But others called them "robber barons." They felt men like Carnegie and Rockefeller made money on the backs of the poor. Leon Czolgosz definitely thought so.

Not all factory workers just sat back and took what was given to them — low wages, long hours, and unsafe working conditions. Workers began organizing into unions. Unions demanded fair pay and better working conditions. If companies didn't agree, the workers could walk off the job and go on strike. Some labor strikes ended peacefully with gains for the workers. Many did not.

On the banks of the Monongahela River in Pennsylvania stood the Homestead Steel Mill. The mill employed 3,800 workers. Every day thousands of workers bustled to and from work. And in July 1892 the mill became the scene of bloodshed.

In June the steel and iron workers union called for a strike. The manager of the mill, Henry Clay Frick (hired by Andrew Carnegie), locked the union strikers out of the plant. He ordered the construction of barbed wire fences around the property.

Striking workers clashed with Pinkerton security guards, who moved in to break the strikers' hold on the Homestead mill.

The strikers formed a ring around the mill. Frick was determined to bring in other workers. But he would need armed guards to do it. So he hired the famed Pinkertons — private security guards — to break through the strikers.

On the night of July 5, some 300 Pinkerton agents gathered downriver, armed with rifles. They assembled onto two barges and made their way upriver, hoping to slip into the mill. They could then escort new, non-union workers into to the mill, and it could reopen.

But all did not go according to plan. On the banks of the river near the mill, 10,000 men, women, and children waited. Many were armed. They weren't going to let the Pinkertons in.

The Pinkertons tried to land, and someone fired a shot. (No one knows if it was the Pinkertons or the strikers). The Pinkertons then opened fire into the crowd. The strikers and the Pinkertons battled all day, until the outnumbered Pinkertons at last surrendered. In all, nine strikers and seven Pinkertons were killed, and many more were wounded. Pennsylvania's governor called in the militia. Eight thousand soldiers showed up, and the mill eventually began running again.

And what does all this have to do with Leon Czolgosz? He wasn't there. He didn't battle the Pinkertons. But something happened afterward that affected him.

On July 23 a man named Alexander Berkman attempted to murder Henry Clay Frick, the manager of Homestead Steel. Berkman was an anarchist.

Enter the Panic of 1893. No, it was not a horror movie. The Panic was a period of economic depression. The price of wheat dropped in early 1893. Then a large company that produced and sold twine went bankrupt. This triggered economic panic, and people began withdrawing money from banks. Many banks collapsed, and companies went bankrupt. Workers lost their jobs. Eventually about 20 percent of Americans were unemployed. Others suffered lower wages. Workers went on strike, and one such worker was Leon Czolgosz. He was part of the 1894 strike at the steel wire mill where he worked.

The United States didn't have enough gold to pay its debts, so President Grover Cleveland turned to a super-rich investor and

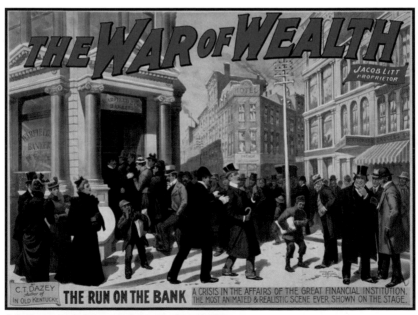

A theater poster depicting a scene from the Panic of 1893

banker named J.P. Morgan for help. Morgan supplied the U.S. with gold to pay its debts. In exchange he received bonds that he could cash in at a later date. (Can you imagine being rich enough to help the United States pay its bills?) Then Morgan got even richer when he eventually cashed in the bonds.

The bailout plan worked. The economy started bouncing back. Banks reopened. Slowly people started getting their jobs back. But unemployment remained high. And across the United States, many workers, farmers, and other people became worried about rich men like J.P. Morgan having control over the government.

Then came the presidential election of 1896: Republican William McKinley vs. Democrat William Jennings Bryan. Bryan ran on an idea called "Free Silver." He said the United States should allow silver to be mined and minted for money in addition to gold. This would help avoid another gold crisis. And it would put more money into circulation. Bryan blamed the United States government for having a limited amount of gold, which limited the money supply, causing the depression.

Rich businessmen like Carnegie, Morgan, and Rockefeller donated money to McKinley's campaign. A man named Mark Hanna ran McKinley's campaign, and Hanna spent five times more money than the Bryan campaign. He brought nearly 750,000 voters to hear McKinley speak from the front porch during the campaign, even arranging for discounted fares on railroads.

The Democrats had a tough challenge that year. Many people blamed Democrat Grover Cleveland for the Panic of 1893. Clearly many voters were not anxious to give another Democrat the

White House. Bryan faced an uphill climb, but he had the support of many rural states.

McKinley, on the other hand, had the support of urban areas in addition to the backing of titans of business. He won the election with 51 percent of the popular vote. Bryan received 47 percent of the popular vote. With 271 electoral votes versus Bryan's 176, McKinley had a victory that pleased the so-called robber barons.

McKinley forged ahead and enjoyed presidential successes: The economy continued to grow, and the Spanish-American war victory turned the United States into an empire with territories across the Western Hemisphere. With Theodore Roosevelt at his side, McKinley won a second showdown with William Jennings Bryan in 1900. And that brings us to the Buffalo World's Fair, and the fateful day that changed everything.

President McKinley in Buffalo, delivering his last public speech.

CHAPTER 4
THE CRIME

Cannon fire shook the ground. Windows of the train car shattered as one cannon after another blasted through the early evening sky. Ida McKinley gasped and clutched her husband's hand. As usual, President McKinley soothed her. The cannons were welcoming them to Buffalo, a thunderous salute. Throngs of admirers clamored toward the train as it rolled through Buffalo and toward the fairgrounds. At the station, the train slowed to a stop. President McKinley stepped out.

A large crowd had gathered. One certain young man pushed his way toward the front of the onlookers. He carried a revolver in his pocket. And he meant to use it.

But the guards held the crowd back. By the time the young man — Leon Czolgosz, no surprise — got to the front, he'd lost his chance. McKinley was already being shuffled into a carriage bound for the fairgrounds.

Czolgosz would have to try again tomorrow.

A week earlier Leon Czolgosz had been far away in Chicago. Out of work, he had been meandering for several months. He was tired of living at home with his family and cruel stepmother. His family was tired of him too. Leon was always asking for money. And he was convinced he was dying.

He thought moving to a warm climate would help him to feel better. He told his brother he wanted to move out West. His brother asked why, and Leon answered, "I can't stand it any longer." Finally the family gathered enough money to get him started on his new life in the West. He left without saying goodbye.

But he didn't go to warmer climes. Instead he went to Chicago and Cleveland, hoping to join anarchist groups. He introduced himself as Fred Nieman (remember Fred "Nobody"?) and asked if they had any secret plots. Immediately the local anarchists dismissed him as a government spy.

Czolgosz continued moving around. While in Chicago again, he saw an interesting newspaper article. The article announced that McKinley was headed to Buffalo, New York, for the Pan-American Exposition. Surely he would tour the fair and give a speech.

That very day Czolgosz bought a train ticket to Buffalo.

★ ★ ★

Czolgosz arrived in Buffalo without a plan. He knew he wanted to show Emma Goldman and the anarchists that he was committed to the cause. But how? After some thinking, it became clear to him. People were converging on Buffalo to see the president. Everyone seemed to be bowing to the great ruler. He made up his mind to kill the great ruler. He would assassinate McKinley. "It was in my heart. There was no escape for me," he said later.

On the day McKinley was due to arrive in Buffalo, Czolgosz went to a hardware store and bought a .32-caliber Iver Johnson revolver, the very same type of gun used in King Umberto's assassination in Italy. Czolgosz still didn't have much of a scheme. His only plan was to follow McKinley around, and surely he'd find the right moment. That evening he went to the train platform at the fairgrounds to wait for McKinley's arrival.

But he'd blown his chance. The crowd was too big. There were too many guards. No matter, though. The president was giving a speech tomorrow. Maybe then he'd get his chance.

Czolgosz woke early. Today would be the day, he thought. He headed quickly to the fairgrounds, hoping to get a good spot. Other people, excited to see the popular president, were already there. Czolgosz got as close a spot as he could. Then he waited.

President McKinley arrived in an open carriage, his wife at his side. A throng of people cheered as he stepped to the podium. "I am glad to again be in the city of Buffalo," he began.

In the crowd Czolgosz tried to push forward. But the gathering was thick, and he couldn't move an inch. He wondered whether he could possibly shoot the president from such a distance. He decided he had to get closer. But he couldn't move.

As the president spoke, Czolgosz sweated. Someone elbowed him. Another person stepped on his foot. How could he possibly get off a good shot with so many people pushing and shoving? *Now,* he told himself.

But the president's speech ended. Security guards whisked McKinley from the stage.

I'll have another chance, Czolgosz thought. *Tomorrow.*

William McKinley wanted to see Niagara Falls. The falls, after all, powered the electricity that lit up the World's Fair. And it was only about an hour from Buffalo. On September 6, the morning after his speech, he got up early and took his usual morning walk. Then he and Ida boarded the train bound for Niagara Falls.

McKinley was stunned by the magnificent falls. He climbed to the highest rock overlooking the falls and gazed at the scenery. Then he and his wife enjoyed a long lunch at a restaurant with a great view.

But time was ticking. McKinley had to be back in Buffalo by 4 p.m. He was scheduled to go to the Temple of Music, where he planned to shake hands with his constituents — the common folk, the typical fairgoers. His personal secretary, George Cortelyou, warned him it was dangerous. But McKinley insisted. He wanted to meet his voters one by one.

McKinley headed back to Buffalo. He had no idea that a man with a gun was waiting for him.

Sometime that day Czolgosz saw in the newspaper that the president would be meeting his voters in the Temple of Music at 4 p.m. It was a perfect opportunity.

Leon headed to the Temple. He made sure his gun was loaded, and he wrapped a white handkerchief around his hand to hide the weapon. That way it would look like he had a bandaged hand. He got in line and waited his turn.

The Temple of Music filled with sound. An organist played classical songs. People in line chatted with each other. President

President McKinley was photographed as he arrived at the Temple of Music, shortly before Czolgosz approached him with a gun in hand.

McKinley wore a huge smile as he greeted each person.

But Leon Czolgosz didn't smile or talk. He simply waited, trying not to look suspicious. He kept his bandaged hand out of sight.

Finally, it was his turn.

McKinley leaned forward with a smile. He reached to shake the young man's hand. Then he noticed the bandage, so he reached for the other hand.

Czolgosz calmly raised the pistol, still wrapped in a white handkerchief, and aimed at McKinley's torso. He fired twice. One bullet slammed into McKinley's chest and the other into his stomach.

Czolgosz fired twice from close range before a bystander tackled him.

A puff of blue smoke rose over the crowd. A stunned and confused McKinley stood still for a split second. What had just happened? Then his cheeks paled. He clutched his chest and lurched backward.

Leon took aim again. But the tall man behind him tackled him and punched him in the neck. Then security guards pounced on him, pummeling him. Fists flew. Shouts rose. Through it all, Czolgosz yelled, "I done my duty!"

And what of McKinley? He was swaying and staggering, blood darkening his white shirt. His secretary, Cortelyou, helped him to a chair. McKinley noticed the young man being beaten to death. "Easy with him, boys!" he ordered.

Guards dragged Leon away. The president noticed the blood now pouring from his stomach. "My wife," he gasped. "Be careful, Cortelyou, how you tell her."

Leon Czolgosz was taken to jail. And President McKinley was carried away in an ambulance. In the ambulance McKinley reached inside his shirt and pulled a bullet from his chest. But there was still another bullet, lodged deep inside his abdomen.

In jail, the shooter told police his name was Nieman. Later, though, he admitted his name was Leon Czolgosz. And he seemed proud of what he'd done.

"I am an anarchist," Czolgosz said. "I killed President McKinley because I done my duty. I don't believe in one man having so much service and another man having none."

San Francisco Chronicle.

VOL. LXXIV.   SAN FRANCISCO, CAL., SATURDAY, SEPTEMBER 7, 1901—SIXTEEN PAGES.   NO. 54.

PRESIDENT M'KINLEY SHOT BY AN ANARCHIST AT BUFFALO FAIR.

Two Bullets Fired by the Assassin, but Only One Penetrates the Body—Surgeons Hopeful of Recovery—An Attempt Made to Lynch the Cowardly Murderer.

WOUNDED AT A PUBLIC RECEPTION.

Stricken by a Man Who Grasped His Hand---Crowd Sought to Mete Out Swift Punishment.

A RECENT PORTRAIT OF PRESIDENT M'KINLEY.

DOCTORS DECLARE INJURIES SEVERE.

The Chances of Recovery Said to Be Against President---Cheering Reports Untrue.

FAVORABLE REPORT ON PRESIDENT'S CONDITION

BUFFALO, N. Y., September 7.—At 3 A. M. the following bulletin was issued: The President continues to rest well. Temperature 102.5, pulse 110, respiration 24.

"P. M. RIXEY."

BUFFALO, September 6.—Secretary Cortelyou to-night gave out the following statement: "The following bulletin was issued by the physicians at 7 P. M.:

"CARING FOR THE WOUNDED CHIEF.

Get the Most Out of Your Food

Hood's Sarsaparilla

Newspapers across the country reported on the crime, McKinley's wounds, and hopes he would recover.

But little did Czolgosz know that President McKinley wasn't dead. He was, in fact, very much alive. At the hospital doctors tried to find the other bullet still in McKinley's body. But they couldn't get to it.

An invention unveiled at the World's Fair, just blocks away, could have helped. That invention was the X-ray machine. But the doctors hesitated. They weren't sure the X-ray machine was safe to use. So, they sewed up McKinley's wounds, the bullet still inside him. And he seemed likely to recover nicely.

He did, at first. He left the hospital and went back to the rooms where he was staying. Vice President Teddy Roosevelt was on a camping trip to the Adirondack Mountains when the shooting took place. He headed for Buffalo when he heard about the attack, then got word the president was recovering and returned to the mountains.

McKinley spent the next six days in bed, reading and sleeping. Ida sat by his side. He was cheerful and a bit lonely. He just wanted to get back to work. But the bullet still inside him was turning to poison. Gangrene grew around the bullet. And then blood poisoning set in. At 2:15 a.m. on September 14, 1901, President McKinley died.

Now Leon Czolgosz, the assassin, could be charged with murder.

President McKinley's casket in the rotunda of the U.S. Capitol

CHAPTER 5
THE AFTERMATH

More than 350 miles away, Theodore Roosevelt leaned back, took a bite of his sandwich, and enjoyed the misty view from Mount Marcy, the highest peak in the Adirondack Mountains and one of the most remote areas in New York State. Suddenly a figure appeared through the mist. A park ranger came running toward Roosevelt's group with a telegram in his hand. Roosevelt read it, his stomach turning. "The President is critically ill," the telegram read. "Absolutely no hope."

Stunned, Roosevelt sat down and finished his sandwich. Then he began the long trek down the mountain. At the bottom he received more news. McKinley was certain to die. And he, Roosevelt, would definitely become the next president.

Roosevelt knew he had to reach Buffalo as soon as possible. He traveled all night in a horse-drawn stagecoach in the rain. The trail was steep and winding, and the horses

Czolgosz behind bars

often slipped. But still, the Roosevelt party galloped on toward the nearest rail depot. A train carried him to Buffalo, where he took the oath of office and became the 26th President of the United States, a president unlike any the nation had ever seen.

Leon Czolgosz stood no chance. Minutes after the shooting, crowds surrounded the Temple of Music, shouting, "Kill him! Kill him!" In the days following, angry mobs formed at the jail. And when President McKinley died, the cries grew louder. The public wanted him executed for what he'd done.

But first, detectives had to figure out if Czolgosz acted alone, or if he was part of a conspiracy. During questioning, Czolgosz said that Emma Goldman's words "set him on fire."

Authorities immediately arrested Goldman in Chicago. They also arrested more than a dozen who worked for her anarchist newspaper *Free Society*. Goldman declared she had nothing to do with the assassination, but she admired it. She was later released due to lack of evidence against her. Several years later she was deported and sent back to Russia.

Leon Czolgosz was the son of immigrants, and his actions caused public outcry against immigration. People became suspicious of immigrants, especially those who had anarchist

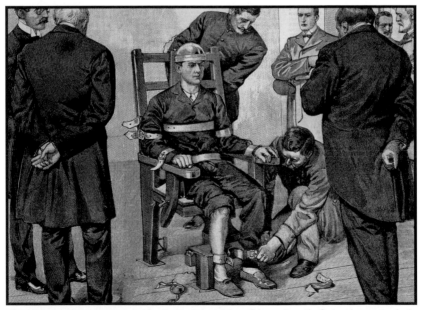

After his trial Czolgosz was executed by electric chair at Auburn Prison, where the first such execution had been carried out about a decade earlier.

or revolutionary ideas. In 1903 Congress passed a law banning immigrants with anarchist backgrounds from entering the country. Fear of anarchy led to various surveillance or spy programs, and the Federal Bureau of Investigation (FBI) was formed in 1908.

During the trial Czolgosz's lawyers defended him by using the insanity plea. They declared that no sane man would attempt to kill the president in broad daylight. Czolgosz had hardly spoken to them, so their case was difficult. And the assassin refused to speak in court. The trial lasted only two days. The jury declared Czolgosz guilty. He was sentenced to death by electric chair.

Czolgosz was transferred to Auburn State Prison in Auburn, New York. Crowds hurled insults as the train carrying Czolgosz passed by. When the train arrived, a mob rushed at him. Guards had to push the crowd back as they dragged him into the prison. Czolgosz was terrified, screaming, "Save me!"

On October 29 the prison warden entered Czolgosz's cell and read him the death warrant. Leon was trembling so violently on the way to the electric chair that guards had to carry him. Once he was strapped in, Czolgosz yelled, "I killed the president for the good of the laboring people, the good people."

Teddy Roosevelt, compared to his predecessors, was young, energetic, and athletic. At 42, he became the youngest president in U.S. history. An outdoorsman, he loved to ride horses, hike, and hunt. On one hunting trip, he refused to shoot a bear cub. A toymaker heard the story and began making small stuffed bears.

Theodore Roosevelt became the youngest person to serve as president, and he approached the job with vigor and determination.

You've probably cuddled one of these. They are called "teddy" bears.

Roosevelt thought the president's mansion needed a name, so he officially dubbed it the White House, which had long been its nickname. He loved to box, and he held boxing matches in his new home. During one bout, he lost his sight in one eye. But that didn't deter him from his visions of the future.

At first he promised to follow McKinley's ideas. But soon

it became clear that he was set on reforming government and politics. He didn't stick to the same old way that things had been done for years. He got rid of corrupt officials and appointed young, college-educated people to his administration.

Roosevelt followed his famous mantra, "Speak softly and carry a big stick." That means, in general, not to start conflicts but be able to defend yourself and use force if you have to. He built up the military and turned the U.S. Navy into the best in the world.

Roosevelt had dreams of expanding trade between the Atlantic and Pacific Oceans. The best way to do that was to build a canal through Central America so ships could pass through, from one ocean to the other. The best site was in Panama. A few years earlier, McKinley's secretary of state, John Hay, had negotiated

A scene from the construction of the Panama Canal

a treaty to allow for construction of a waterway connecting the oceans. Roosevelt was determined to see the project through. Construction on the Panama Canal began in 1904 and went on for a decade.

Some very rich men were scared of Roosevelt's presidency. Remember Andrew Carnegie and John D. Rockefeller? Those guys weren't exactly excited that he'd come to power. Roosevelt was antitrust, which meant he wanted to break up big industrial corporations — or trusts — and monopolies. Small businesses were suffering, and Roosevelt wanted to change that. His antitrust ideas were the exact opposite of McKinley's. He became a "trust buster" and brought lawsuits against many large corporations.

In 1902 a major coal miner strike shook the country. The mine owners refused to offer higher wages and better conditions, so the miners refused to go back to work. The nation now faced a coal shortage. Teddy Roosevelt stepped in and threatened that the government would take over the coal mines. The mine owners then agreed to meet the miners' requests. This was the first time a president had ever sided with workers rather than owners. Labor reform still had a long way to go, but Roosevelt's intervention turned the tide toward better treatment of workers.

Roosevelt ran for president in 1904 and won easily. One of his first causes in his second term was to ensure food was safe to eat. New laws made sure food, especially meat, was inspected before being sold. This led to the creation of a federal agency called the Food and Drug Administration.

Have you ever taken a spelling test? You can thank Teddy Roosevelt for that. Before his presidency, there was no standard, correct spelling of many words. In 1906 the Simplified Spelling Board was created by a guy we've heard of before — Andrew Carnegie. Carnegie aimed to simplify spelling so English was easier to read and learn. Roosevelt supported the idea and gave an order that the government must use the board's spelling rules.

Some of Teddy Roosevelt's greatest accomplishments were in conservation. He loved the outdoors, and he was concerned that human development would take over natural areas. So he set aside nearly 200 million acres for national parks and wildlife refuges. Without Teddy Roosevelt, we might not be able to visit the Grand Canyon or camp in Glacier National Park in Montana. And some say that without Leon Czolgosz, we wouldn't have these parks either.

Roosevelt's presidency ended in 1909, and he set out for a 10-month African safari. When he returned, he discovered he didn't like what the current president, Howard Taft, was doing. So he decided to run for president again in 1912. The Republican Party didn't nominate him, so he created his own party, the Progressive Party, nicknamed the "Bull Moose" Party.

Why Bull Moose? Here's an interesting story: After McKinley's assassination, a man named John Schrank had a dream. In his dream the ghost of President McKinley appeared. The ghost pointed to a picture of Teddy Roosevelt and said, "This is my murderer. Avenge my death." So, in 1912, Schrank followed Roosevelt on the campaign trail. In Milwaukee, Wisconsin, Roosevelt was preparing to make a speech. He stepped out of a hotel, and Schrank shot him. The bullet passed through Roosevelt's fifty-page written speech and lodged in his chest. But Roosevelt didn't go to the doctor. He went on to give his 90-minute speech, saying that "It takes more than [one bullet] to kill a Bull Moose."

Roosevelt didn't win the election. He finished second, and Taft finished third. Roosevelt received the largest number of third-party votes in history. The presidency went to Democrat Woodrow Wilson. Wilson actually adopted many of Roosevelt's progressive ideas. He continued antitrust ideas and labor reform. Progressive reforms continued under another Roosevelt, Teddy's fifth cousin Franklin Delano Roosevelt, who became president in 1933.

William McKinley's presidency was overshadowed by Teddy Roosevelt. Many historians consider Roosevelt one of the top five presidents in history, but McKinley has largely been forgotten. Even the nation's tallest mountain, once called Mount McKinley, has had its previous name, Denali, restored. But remember that he was popular in his time. So, what might have happened if Leon Czolgosz hadn't killed McKinley? What would the nation have been like?

McKinley probably would not have set aside land for national parks and forests. McKinley wasn't moved by nature in the way Roosevelt was. Swaths of that land probably would have been mined, trees would've been chopped down, and houses and businesses would've been built. If you wanted to see the Grand Canyon, you might have had to trespass on private property for a glimpse.

And McKinley most certainly wouldn't have supported antitrust laws. Historians suggest large monopolies would have continued under his presidency. They say the gap between rich and poor would have continued to widen. Those things are perhaps true. But Leon Czolgosz wasn't the only one upset about the rich getting richer and the poor getting poorer. Many Americans were seeking change without violence. The public probably would have called for reforms like the trust-busting, even without Teddy Roosevelt.

Theodore Roosevelt often gets the credit for strengthening the nation's military, but McKinley had already set the idea in motion. Under McKinley the United States grew into an empire and a world power, so a strong military was in McKinley's sights. And the Panama Canal was within his sights too. The French were already starting to build it, and they had asked for America's help. The Senate would have voted to support it, no matter who was president.

Some people even say Czolgosz's crime cleared the way for progressive reform. Maybe these reforms would have happened without murder, maybe they would've come much later or in different forms, or maybe not at all. But history can't be rewritten. The facts remain. In 1901 a disgruntled man with a hidden gun killed our president. Those bullets rang in the end of the old and the beginning of the new. The 20th century dawned, and with it a fiery, young, new president who made lasting changes. Today we can still hear the echo of Leon Czolgosz's gunshots.

Denali, a mountain in Alaska, is the highest peak in North America. It was called Mount McKinley from 1917 to 2015.

TIMELINE ›››››››››››››››››››››››››

Jan. 29, 1843: William McKinley is born in Niles, Ohio

Sept. 17, 1862: McKinley performs heroic act of bringing rations to soldiers during the Battle of Antietam

May 5, 1873: Leon Czolgosz is born in Alpena, Michigan, to Polish immigrant parents

1893: An economic crash hits the nation; Leon Czolgosz takes part in a workers' strike and is fired

Nov. 3, 1896: Republican William McKinley wins the presidential election

March 4, 1897: McKinley is sworn in as the nation's 25th president

1898: Leon Czolgosz quits his job and moves in with his family; he becomes interested in anarchy

Feb. 15, 1898: USS *Maine* explodes in Havana Harbor

April 25, 1898: War is formally declared between the United States and Spain

Dec. 10, 1898: The Spanish-American War ends with the signing of the Treaty of Paris between the U.S. and Spain

July 29, 1900: Italy's King Umberto I is assassinated

Nov. 6, 1900: William McKinley is elected to serve a second term as president

May 1, 1901: The World's Fair — called the Pan-American Exposition — opens in Buffalo

May 6, 1901: Czolgosz hears Emma Goldman speak

Aug. 31, 1901: Czolgosz goes to Buffalo, New York, and rents a room

Sept. 4, 1901: President McKinley arrives in Buffalo

Sept. 5, 1901: Czolgosz attends President McKinley's speech

Sept. 6, 1901: Czolgosz shoots President McKinley twice — once in the chest and once in the abdomen

Sept. 14, 1901: President McKinley dies of his wounds; Theodore Roosevelt takes the oath of office and becomes president

Sept. 23, 1901: Czolgosz goes on trial for the murder of William McKinley; Czolgosz is convicted and sentenced to death

Oct. 29, 1901: Leon Czolgosz is executed by electric chair

Oct. 14, 1912: Theodore Roosevelt is shot while on the campaign trail but is not seriously injured

1914: The Panama Canal is completed

1919: Anarchist Emma Goldman is deported to Russia

GLOSSARY

anarchy—a system of no government

capitalism—economic system that allows people to freely create businesses and own as much property as they can afford

economy— the way a country produces, distributes, and uses its money, goods, natural resources, and services

empire—a group of countries or lands under one government or ruler

exposition—a public exhibition or show

industrial— having to do with a type of business or manufacturing

monopoly—situation in which there is only one supplier of a good or service, and therefore that supplier can control the price and the market

strike—the refusal to work because of a disagreement with the employer over wages or working conditions

territories—lands and waters under control of a nation or ruler

textile—woven cloth or fabric

trust—separate companies that join to limit competition by controlling production and distribution of products and services

union—an organized group of workers that tries to gain better pay and working conditions for workers

SOURCE NOTES

Page 6, line 9: McKinley, William. *President McKinley's Last Speech*. New York: Henry Malkan, 1901.

Page 13, line 17: Miller, Scott. *The President and the Assassin: McKinley, Terror, and Empire at the Dawn of the American Century*. New York: Random House, 2011, p. 109.

Page 38, line 8: Ibid., p. 283.

Page 39, line 5: Ibid., p. 297.

Page 39, line 22: *President McKinley's Last Speech*.

Page 43, line 8: *The President and the Assassin: McKinley, Terror, and Empire at the Dawn of the American Century*, p. 301.

Page 43, line 12: Rauchway, Eric. *Murdering McKinley: The Making of Theodore Roosevelt's America*. New York: Farrar, Straus, and Giroux, 2003, p. 3.

Page 43, line 14: *The President and the Assassin: McKinley, Terror, and Empire at the Dawn of the American Century*, p. 302.

Page 43, line 23: *Murdering McKinley: The Making of Theodore Roosevelt's America*, p. 19.

Page 47, line 7: Vowell, Sarah. *Assassination Vacation*. New York: Simon & Schuster, 2005, p. 227.

Page 50, line 15: *The President and the Assassin: McKinley, Terror, and Empire at the Dawn of the American Century*, p. 328.

Page 50, line 19: Ibid, p. 330.

Page 54, line 23: "Who Shot T.R.?" National Park Service. 20 April 2017. October 2017.https://www.nps.gov/thrb/learn/historyculture/whoshottr.htm

Page 55, line 2: Ibid.

SELECT BIBLIOGRAPHY

Clarke, James W. *American Assassins: The Darker Side of Politics*. Princeton, N.J.: Princeton University Press, 1982.

Creighton, Margaret. *The Electrifying Rise and Fall of Rainbow City: Spectacle and Assassination at the 1901 World's Fair*. New York: W.W. Norton & Company, 2016.

Halstead, Murat. *The Illustrious Life of William McKinley, Our Martyred President*. Chicago: Murat Halstead, 1901.

Lindop, Edmund. *Assassinations that Shook America*. New York: Franklin Watts, 1992.

McKinley, William. *President McKinley's Last Speech*. New York: Henry Malkan, 1901.

Miller, Scott. *The President and the Assassin: McKinley, Terror, and Empire at the Dawn of the American Century*. New York: Random House, 2011.

Rauchway, Eric. *Murdering McKinley: The Making of Theodore Roosevelt's America*. New York: Farrar, Straus, and Giroux, 2003.

Rove, Karl. *The Triumph of William McKinley: Why the Election of 1896 Still Matters*. New York: Simon & Schuster, 2015.

Vowell, Sarah. *Assassination Vacation*. New York: Simon & Schuster, 2005.

Williams, R. Hal. *Realigning America: McKinley, Bryan, and the Remarkable Election of 1896*. Lawrence, KS: University Press of Kansas, 2010.

"Who Shot T.R.?" National Park Service. 20 April 2017. October 2017.https://www.nps.gov/thrb/learn/historyculture/whoshottr.htm

ADDITIONAL RESOURCES

READ MORE

Bailey, Diane. *William McKinley: The 25th President*. New York: Bearport Publishing, 2017.

Barber, James. *Presidents*. New York: DK Publishing, 2017.

Carlson-Berne, Emma. *The Presidency of Theodore Roosevelt: Leading from the Bully Pulpit*. North Mankato, Minn.: Compass Point Books, 2015.

Gunderson, Megan M. *William McKinley*. Minneapolis: Abdo Publishing, 2016.

Mahoney, Emily. *The Industrial Revolution: The Birth of Modern America*. San Diego: Lucent Books, 2017.

INTERNET SITES

Use FactHound to find Internet sites related to this book.

Visit www.facthound.com

Just type in 9780756557140 and go.

INDEX

ABOUT THE AUTHOR

JESSICA GUNDERSON

grew up in the small town of Washburn, North Dakota. She has a bachelor's degree from the University of North Dakota and an MFA in Creative Writing from Minnesota State University, Mankato. She has written more than seventy-five books for young readers. An avid enthusiast of Civil War history and Abraham Lincoln, she is the author of *The Election of 1860: A Nation Divides on the Eve of War* and *The Wound is Mortal: The Story of the Assassination of Abraham Lincoln*. She currently lives in Madison, Wisconsin, with her husband and cat.

PHOTO CREDITS